Star Now Book ©

THIS Book BELONGS TO:

....

....

welcome to fashion coloring book

FUN COLORING

www.ingramcontent.com/pod-product-compliance
Lightning Source LLC
Chambersburg PA
CBHW082117220526
45472CB00009B/2206
* 9 7 9 8 6 8 2 0 4 4 7 9 5 *